Integrity ... Relationships ... Credibility ... Reputation ...
Negotiation ... Listening ... Entrepreneurialism ... Money ...
Productivity ... Time ... Confrontation ... Leadership

12 TIME-TESTED PRINCIPLES FOR A
LIFETIME OF PROSPERITY AND SUCCESS

Integrity

#27: Get rid of anything less than excellent in your life, and your integrity will increase.

Credibility

#61: The more your certainty and confidence outweigh your doubts, the more people will believe in you.

Leadership

#338: Leaders trust and believe in their instincts because they are frequently providing a vision of a future that doesn't yet exist.

Productivity

#270: If you want a list of all the bottlenecks or capacity blocks in your organization, have your staff make a list of everything they least like to do.

Confrontation

#318: Forget about what you did yesterday. Your employer is more interested in what you will do today and tomorrow.

#333: Circumstances are not a valid excuse for a lack of performance. If you cannot confront and overcome your circumstances, your performance will suffer.

Whether you are an investor, a corporate executive, or self-employed, *365 Ways to Become a Millionaire* will create breakthrough results in all areas of your life and give you the tools you need to achieve your business goals.

365 WAYS TO BECOME A MILLIONAIRE

BRIAN KOSLOW became a self-made millionaire at age thirty-one. During the past twenty-one years as an executive coach and business growth strategist, Brian has helped thousands of individuals and companies to grow exponentially and increase their income. Moreover, during this time he concurrently founded and developed three profitable multi-million-dollar companies.

Brian provides live teleconferences and seminars each month that are dedicated to helping people throughout the world who are ready to make the commitment to do what is necessary to become multimillionaires.

Currently, Brian is an executive coach and business growth strategist who makes his home in Florida. If you would like to hire Brian to speak to your company or organization, please visit www.mystrategiccoach.com.

$$$ 365 $$$

Ways to Become a

Millionaire

(Without Being Born One)

REVISED AND UPDATED

Brian Koslow

A PLUME BOOK

PLUME
Published by Penguin Group
Penguin Group (USA) Inc., 375 Hudson Street, New York, New York 10014, U.S.A. • Penguin
Group (Canada), 90 Eglinton Avenue East, Suite 700, Toronto, Ontario, Canada M4P 2Y3 (a divi-
sion of Pearson Penguin Canada Inc.) • Penguin Books Ltd., 80 Strand, London WC2R ORL, En-
gland. • Penguin Ireland, 25 St. Stephen's Green, Dublin 2, Ireland (a division of Penguin Books
Ltd.) • Penguin Group (Australia), 250 Camberwell Road, Camberwell, Victoria 3124, Australia
(a division of Pearson Australia Group Pty. Ltd.) • Penguin Books India Pvt. Ltd., 11 Community
Centre, Panchsheel Park, New Delhi – 110 017, India • Penguin Group (NZ), 67 Apollo Drive,
Rosedale, North Shore 0745, Auckland, New Zealand (a division of Pearson New Zealand Ltd.) •
Penguin Books (South Africa) (Pty.) Ltd., 24 Sturdee Avenue, Rosebank, Johannesburg 2196,
South Africa

Penguin Books Ltd., Registered Offices: 80 Strand, London WC2R 0RL, England

First published by Plume, a member of Penguin Group (USA) Inc.

First Printing, October 1999
First Printing (revised edition), January 2008
10 9 8 7 6 5 4 3 2 1

 REGISTERED TRADEMARK – MARCA REGISTRADA

LIBRARY OF CONGRESS CATALOGING-IN-PUBLICATION DATA
Koslow, Brian.
365 ways to become a millionaire : (without being born one) / Brian Koslow.
p. cm.
ISBN 978-0-452-28896-6
  1. Success in business. I. Title. II. Title: Three hundred sixty-five ways to become a millionaire
     (without being born one)
HF5386.K7755   2007
332.024'01—dc22   2007014368
CIP

Printed in the United States of America
Set in Palatino and Birch
Designed by Eve L. Kirch

To my father, whose presence is with me every day. He was the most important mentor and teacher of all. He taught me that relationships are the foundation of everything. He exemplified love, forgiveness, and trust. He acted with integrity and was a source of wisdom and compassion to others. He was a brilliant businessman and wonderful father.

CONTENTS

ix

Contents

Contents

FOREWORD

MY name is Martin Cohen, and I am a professional coach to corporations and executives. For the past twenty years, I have coached a wide array of highly successful people across many professions and industries. Among those people, there have been many millionaires. I have known Brian Koslow personally for more than ten years. Brian is a coach's dream. He has been, and remains, a client and friend, in what I would consider to be a lifelong relationship.

I am deeply honored to express my feelings on the unique contribution Brian has made. Brian personifies the possibility of abundance in the new millennium and has successfully incorporated an insightful set of principles into his career as an entrepreneur and public speaker. His principles, which are beautifully expressed in this book, are a dream come true for anyone who wants to expand his or her wealth, success, and personal fulfillment.

Brian's willingness to surrender and adhere to the principles in this book is what has allowed him and his clients to know what it is to be wealthy in every sense of the word. Through his skill and intention, he not only creates exciting possibilities for people and their businesses but also lives what he professes. To be in his presence is both informative and inspirational.

Brian is living proof that anything is possible. The key to achieving the level of success that Brian has created is based on the degree to which you are willing to open yourself up to Brian's principles. I invite you to be receptive to the wisdom of Brian's principles and allow the words you read in this book to coach you toward a future of prosperity and abundance.

> —Martin Cohen
> Martin Cohen Consultants, Inc.
> New York City

SHARE THE WISDOM

Thanks to you, *365 Ways to Become a Millionaire (Without Being Born One)* has been published in five languages and has had a positive impact throughout the world. Brian Koslow is committed to you living life to your fullest capabilities. With the principles in his book, Brian has set the groundwork for you to move forward powerfully, shedding negativity, burdens, and guilt so that you can seize opportunities and take effective action.

Becoming a millionaire is all about increasing your effectiveness. Brian teaches that the more effective you become, the more you claim your power to cause the results you want, rather than being at the effect of your circumstances. It is all up to you! You must start with a commitment to be a bigger demand on yourself, to expect more and deliver, just because *you* said so. Moreover, being highly effective will have you leading in your work, home, communities, and in the world.

As you become more effective and generate greater results in your life, you will experience your influence to powerfully inspire others. That opportunity is the gift of the millionaire, sharing millionaire principles so others can recognize and expand their own potential.

Brian has provided you with *365 Ways to Become a Millionaire (Without Being Born One)*—a book with compelling perspectives that can be an empowering gift to pass on to others. One person at a time, you and Brian can work together to expand people's potential and fulfill their destiny. The difference that you make for others will be rewarded throughout your lifetime.

Live, prosper, and share the wisdom.

—Dr. Meryl Koslow, D.C.
Vice President/Cofounder
Strategic Coaching, Inc.

ACKNOWLEDGMENTS

M<small>Y</small> wife, Meryl, continually provides me with the trust and encouragement I need to take risks, fail, succeed, and learn. She is an endless supply of endorsement and vision. I acknowledge her for her commitment to our relationship and our family.

To my mentors: Jack Taub, an entrepreneur who shared his life with me for three years, during nearly every waking moment. Jack taught me more about risk taking, leveraging, and listening than anyone I know. I should have paid him for all the time he paid me. And to Frank Trumbower, a brilliant investment banker and leader who taught me about planning, implementing, strategizing, and communicating. He gave me the freedom to fail and the guidance to succeed. He taught me how to believe in people.

To my special friend Michael Fishman, without whom this book would have never been in your hands. Michael is a marketing genius and a gigantic contribution to others.

To my literary agent, Sheree Bykofsky, and my editor, Laurie Viera. Your talent, wisdom, and around-the-clock work ethics are deeply appreciated. Your teamwork has provided the guidance to make this book possible, and your encouragement has germinated the seeds for my next book. You are both gifts to the literary profession.

To my sister-in-law, Katie, for her comments, review, and question marks. Katie helped make the complex simple and organized the manuscript into its present format. Katie also took care of the multitude of administrative and secretarial details that are essential ingredients in bringing this book to you. Katie is a total joy to work with.

Acknowledgments

I also acknowledge each of my clients for the opportunity to serve them. Through their commitments and inspiration, they have proved the principles in this book. I am grateful to each of you for your vulnerability, for entrusting my staff and me with your businesses, and for sharing your deepest concerns and your grandest visions. I sincerely acknowledge you for your courage to act and to do what is necessary to make a difference in the world.

> —Brian M. Koslow
> President/CEO
> Strategic Coaching, Inc.
> www.mystrategiccoach.com

AUTHOR'S NOTE

THANK you for choosing this book. My sincere hope is that the coaching I have provided herein will make a profound and lasting difference for you, your business, and your family.

Over the past twenty-one years, thousands of people have utilized the insights in this book to become more effective, expand their possibilities, and create breakthroughs for themselves. The contents of this book are neither hypothetical nor theoretical; instead, they are insights that have a proven track record of powerful and positive results.

I have divided the book into twelve sections, each structured to provide you with unique and valuable insights into your own potential. You may use this book as a reference for contemplation, guidance, or for daily affirmation.

Whether you are an executive leader, politician, manager, salesperson, secretary, or laborer, I dedicate this book to you. I sincerely acknowledge you for your courage to take risks and your willingness to embrace change. May you experience the rewards that result from living life at your highest level of effectiveness.

—Brian M. Koslow
President/CEO
Strategic Coaching, Inc.
www.mystrategiccoach.com

$$$ 365 $$$

Ways to Become a

Millionaire

(Without Being Born One)

$$$$$$$
Integrity

R ECENTLY, I was presenting a seminar on the subject of integrity to a group of professionals. It was remarkable to learn how many different interpretations there could be for one word. Perhaps most fascinating were the many personal reactions that were brought out in each participant. This hot topic had all of the attendees assessing their own integrity—which is about personal wholeness, consistency, authenticity, and commitment to values and principles—in all of their daily interactions and activities.

In one of the exercises, we asked the participants to write down instances in which they felt they might have compromised their integrity in the past, and those in which they suspected their integrity might still be at risk. Interestingly, most participants were able to find one or more customary activities in which their integrity was indeed compromised. However, once the participants evaluated the rewards and risks associated with compromising their integrity, they consistently concluded that the inevitable, long-term negative results overshadowed the appeal of the short-term gains. Without a doubt, integrity is directly related to producing consistent, long-term effectiveness and positive results.

$$ 1 $$

ALWAYS keep your word. If a change in circumstances means that keeping your word would be life threatening or otherwise devastating, renegotiate with the intent of maintaining your integrity.

$$ 2 $$

INTEGRITY requires consistency between your public statements and your private thoughts.

$$ 3 $$

HIGHLY effective people never blame circumstances for their lack of results. Instead, they accept responsibility and recommit to the actions necessary to produce the intended results.

$$ 4 $$

FOCUS on giving rather than getting, and you will ultimately attract much greater success.

$$ 5 $$

TREAT people without judgment, and they will more readily support your dreams.

$$ 6 $$

WHEN integrity exists in an organization, people's willingness to be passionately committed will increase. Passionately committed people are the foundation of an organization that consistently produces seemingly impossible results.

$$ 7 $$

HAVE a policy for everything. Policies are what allow an organization to function efficiently. Without policies, you will always get less done, and you will spend more time trying to preserve your organization's integrity.

$$ 8 $$

IF you respond to your circumstances in an ethical and moral manner, and produce results consistent with what you said, you will be considered "outstanding" and attract more opportunities.

$$ 9 $$

A SINGLE employee who does not have integrity can—and sooner or later will—throw off the productivity and integrity of your company and pose a threat to your reputation.

$$ 10 $$

NEVER do anything else while speaking on the telephone. The people listening on the other end will know that your attention is elsewhere and will interpret your actions as disinterest in them and their needs. If you do this repeatedly, your customers will telephone your competitor.

$$ 11 $$

APPLYING one personality for business and another for your "personal life" can be unnecessarily stressful. You will find that being your authentic self at all times—in other words, maintaining a state of wholeness or integrity—will yield you the greatest success.

$$ 12 $$

NEVER judge or underestimate people by their physical appearance. Successful people (who may be willing to invest in you) come in all weights, heights, shapes, sizes, and colors.

$$ 13 $$

IF you consistently do the best you can, with integrity, you will regret less and move forward with greater ease.

$$ 14 $$

YOUR integrity is at stake when your actions don't match your words. Moreover, your reputation, credibility, and relationships are at stake too.

$$ 15 $$

YOUR employees may write what they would never think of telling you out loud. Consider creating a communication form that asks pertinent questions about an employee's individual perspectives. This will help preserve your organization's integrity.

$$ 16 $$

ALWAYS take the most ethical and moral course. Never do anything that will make you lose sleep. In the long run, you will benefit more by doing what is right, even if the immediate cost of doing so is higher.

$$ 17 $$

WHEN an organization has integrity, it can more easily attract and keep competent, talented people. When an organization lacks integrity, competent, talented people will leave.

$$ 18 $$

BREAKING your commitments always results in frustration to the people dependent on you. Never break your commitments unless you responsibly communicate your change in commitment to everyone depending on you.

$$ 19 $$

"Burnout" is not a result of being too busy. It is an indication of a lost sense of purpose and a lack of fulfillment. When both purpose and fulfillment are present, you are in a state of wholeness, and burnout cannot exist.

$$ 20 $$

Any unethical or immoral behavior or attitude is self-sabotaging and repels people. You will attract more success by eliminating it ... even the small transgressions that nobody notices.

$$ 21 $$

IF you run your business based upon personalities, your results will vary with moods and emotions. If you run your business based upon principles, values, and commitments, your efforts will produce more consistent results.

$$ 22 $$

INTEGRITY is taking the high road, even when the alternative is more enticing.

$$ 23 $$

YOU will forgive people more easily when you end your need to make them wrong.

$$ 24 $$

YOUR brain is made up of cells of energy. If you can focus without distractions, your brain cells can be used with the precision of a laser. Successful people have mastered the ability to focus on the issue at hand. Eliminate your distractions and practice increasing your focusing skills. Greater focus on your primary objectives will produce increased effectiveness and allow you to maintain integrity in whatever you do.

$$ 25 $$

NOURISH your body properly. It's the only one you have. Without proper nourishment, your body will not maintain its integrity or wholeness. When was the last time you had a massage, took an anti-oxidant, had fresh vegetable juice, or exercised?

$$ 26 $$

You are not your mind. Your mind is a very small, yet potent, part of you. Control it, focus it, and nourish it with positive thoughts that resonate with your authentic self. Revitalize positively charged brain cells by surrounding yourself with positive people, reading positive books, and listening to positive CDs. Start now! Visit www. 365Ways toBecomeaMillionaire.com and download daily positive "Millionaire Thoughts"!

$$ 27 $$

GET rid of anything less than excellent in your life, and your integrity will increase.

$$ 28 $$

YOU will always know a person's true intentions when you see their results. Integrity exists when the stated intentions and results match.

$$ 29 $$

THE Wizard of Oz was right when he said to believe in ourselves. And the Good Witch of the East was right when she said that most times the answers are already inside of us. Like Dorothy, we must be true to ourselves and allow others to help us reveal the answers that are already inside of us.

$$ 30 $$

IF you would not volunteer to do the job you have, you are probably doing the wrong job.

$$ 31 $$

THE most powerful thing to believe in is yourself and your own abilities.

$$$$$$$$
Relationships

RELATIONSHIPS are a prerequisite for producing results beyond ourselves. They expand our imaginations to infinite possibilities that cannot exist in a life of isolation.

Relationships give meaning to our lives. They are about mutual commitments. Relationships are also the platform for extraordinary results. Through an invisible synergistic energy beyond our individual selves, relationships make opportunities and results possible that could not have otherwise occurred.

$$ 32 $$

TRUST is the foundation of all good relationships.

$$ 33 $$

YOU will get much further ahead in life if you trust people first, rather than mistrust people first.

$$ 34 $$

THE more you complain, the fewer opportunities people will offer you. If you have a complaint, provide a solution to a person who can do something about it.

$$ 35 $$

BEING passionate will increase your magnetic field for attracting others. Oftentimes, it is the primary reason that relatives, friends, and associates will invest in you.

$$ 36 $$

YOUR staff and customers will not be more enthusiastic than you are.

$$ 37 $$

IF your spouse or significant other is supportive of your actions and empowers you, success will come easier to you. My advice: Look upon your relationship with your life partner as sacred.

$$ 38 $$

PARTNERSHIPS will attain the greatest success possible if the partners share a common vision and are willing to eliminate any existing dysfunction.

$$ 39 $$

THE most needed, wanted, and powerful activity in which you can engage on or off the job is to authentically recognize, acknowledge, and appreciate others. It costs you nothing and can unlock the potential in others.

$$ 40 $$

A BAD attitude will get you fired sooner or later, regardless of your skills. A bad attitude is toxic to any organization.

$$ 41 $$

THE more people you influence, the more power you have.

$$ 42 $$

PRACTICE making other people "right." They will feel validated, become more productive, expand, and take more risks.

$$ 43 $$

THE people with whom you choose to spend your time can easily determine how far ahead you get in life.

$$ 44 $$

ONE way to really know if you are excellent is to look around you and see if all of your close relationships are excellent. The one person all of these relationships have in common is you.

$$ 45 $$

IF people don't see what they hear, they will automatically mistrust. Mistrust destroys relationships.

$$ 46 $$

THE moment you blame anyone for anything, your relationship and your personal power deteriorate.

Try this: For one full week, do not blame anyone for anything. You might be surprised to notice how many times you blame others, creating conflict or pushing people away. By eliminating blame, you can move relationships and opportunities forward faster.

$$ 47 $$

THE more you judge people, the more you will push them away.

$$ 48 $$

ATTITUDE can be changed in a nanosecond. People with a positive attitude will attract opportunities more easily, earn more, and have better relationships with their peers.

$$ 49 $$

ENCOURAGE everyone in your company to be in the process of continual self-improvement. Pass a copy of this book to every coworker and employer and to each of your suppliers. They'll appreciate you more.

23

$$ 50 $$

NEVER commiserate with fellow workers. Negative people have no chance of survival in a proactive, profitable company.

$$ 51 $$

To boost employee morale, confidence, and teamwork, make sure you and your company are engaged in ongoing professional coaching.

To find out more about professional coaching for yourself and your business, visit www.mystrateg iccoach.com.

$$ 52 $$

THE stronger your relationships are with customers, the more frequent and higher the dollar amount of your sales. The underlying key to repeat sales is your customer's ongoing relationship with you. To assure that you are maintaining your client relationships in the best manner possible, have a marketing professional review your client retention systems each year.

$$ 53 $$

IF you are never disappointed, your expectations of people are probably not high enough. People will usually perform better when they are surrounded by higher expectations.

$$ 54 $$

Envy, jealousy, and being impressed with other people's money are attitudes that will not earn the respect or favor of those who are on the receiving end.

$$ 55 $$

The art of getting customers to buy is much more effective than the art of selling. Take a genuine interest in your customers, and they will be more likely to *want* to buy from you.

$$ 56 $$

ALWAYS address your business letters to a specific person. Always state exactly why you are writing in the first sentence. Always point out specific benefits to the reader in the first paragraph. Always give the reader the next specific action step to take. Always make it easy for the reader to say "yes" to your next action step. All of the above will give you the opportunity to develop your relationship with the reader and increase your results.

$$ 57 $$

BE generous with your humanity, compassion, and gratefulness. This is a leading cause of miracles.

$$ 58 $$

MORE opportunities will result in any relationship where perfunctory activities are replaced with those driven by an affinity for the other party.

$$ 59 $$

REMEMBER above all else that no business, power, position, wealth, or fame is a substitute for your family.

$$$$$$$$$
Credibility

CREDIBILITY is essential to producing results with ease. A company with credibility is able to introduce new products and services with a demand ready to embrace them. Customers are willing to put their faith in a company that has demonstrated credibility. When credibility is present, customers are buying rather than being sold.

Individuals who have credibility find it unnecessary to convince others. Their credibility has given them magical access to results, because they are able to instantaneously gain the trust and faith of others. Credible people are the trustees of authority. To maintain and expand the authority that others have entrusted in them, they must produce results, which in turn makes them more credible.

$$ 60 $$

MAKE a list of at least three things that are unique about you, your services, and/or your products. Communicate these more frequently, and your value will go up. So will your sales.

$$ 61 $$

THE more your certainty and confidence outweigh your doubts, the more people will believe in you.

$$ 62 $$

THE more responsibility you are willing to accept for your actions, the more credibility you will have.

$$ 63 $$

ALWAYS wear expensive shoes. People notice.

$$ 64 $$

YOU will attract more people to you if you act and speak from abundance rather than scarcity.

$$ 65 $$

IF everybody believed you, you would be selling more.

$$ 66 $$

CREDIBILITY is the underlying foundation of every leader. The root of credibility begins with being honest.

$$ 67 $$

NEVER lie to anyone. Lost credibility is too costly and too difficult to regain.

$$ 68 $$

NEVER use slang words. Never say "yeah"; say "yes." Never say "gonna"; say "going to." Never curse; never show disrespect. All of these things will diminish your credibility and impact your personal profitability.

$$ 69 $$

THE more you respect another person, the more they will trust you.

$$ 70 $$

ACCEPT your weaknesses instead of resisting them, and you will gain more credibility and move forward with greater velocity.

$$ 71 $$

PEOPLE will be resistant to taking a financial risk unless they are presented with an opportunity by someone with credibility. The presenter is therefore more important than the presentation. The messenger is more important than the message.

$$ 72 $$

YOUR personal physiology will affect your confidence, your credibility, and your results over time. For example, your posture tells others if you are confident or burdened. Imagine that a helium balloon is attached to the center of your head, and relax your body. The balloon will lift you up to perfect posture, and you will feel more confident.

$$ 73 $$

PEOPLE don't typically act upon the facts. They tend to *re*act based on their emotional response to the facts. To gain credibility, you must develop objectivity. Do this by responding to the facts instead of reacting to emotional content.

$$ 74 $$

IMPROVE the quality of your handshake. It is an instant barometer of your sense of self-worth and self-esteem and can instantly boost your credibility.

To evaluate your handshake—and improve it— visit www.365WaystoBecomeaMillionaire.com.

$$ 75 $$

THE biggest waste of mental energy is spent on self-criticism. To accomplish more, redirect your mental energy by continuously reminding yourself of all the things you do right. Belief in yourself will increase your confidence and credibility.

$$ 76 $$

YOUR résumé provides an inside-out photograph of your past accomplishments. If you have not added any new skills, talents, or results to it each year, you are stagnating, and someone looking at it will question your credibility.

$$ 77 $$

ABOVE all else, practice what you preach. People must see what they hear, or you will lose credibility.

$$ 78 $$

THE credibility paradox: When you produce results, you gain credibility. When you have credibility, you will have an easier time producing results.

$$ 79 $$

NEVER begin or perpetuate a rumor, gossip, or any negative comments about anyone. All of the above will come back to reduce your personal credibility and profitability.

$$ 80 $$

THE higher your confidence, the faster other people's doubts about you will evaporate.

$$ 81 $$

SURROUND yourself with people who believe in you. It will validate and empower you, making it easier to accomplish your goals.

$$ 82 $$

To increase your credibility, make your emotions subordinate to your commitments.

$$ 83 $$

IN the long run, being honest will generate more employee and customer trust, expand your opportunities, and attract more wealth to you than all of the short-term gains derived from being dishonest.

$$ 84 $$

IF you allow yourself to be dominated or consumed by your circumstances, you will lose credibility. Credibility is directly related to controlling circumstances rather than being controlled by them.

$$ 85 $$

ONE of the most important things to do with any partnership, committee, or team is to resolve any disharmony among its members. This is essential for the team to maximize its credibility and results.

$$ 86 $$

EACH time you shop for clothing, upgrade the quality of your wardrobe. People have a tendency to lend more credibility and respect to a person wearing fine clothes.

$$ 87 $$

A SILENT threat to your credibility is making assumptions. Most assumptions are inaccurate.

$$ 88 $$

NEVER write an order with an inexpensive pen.

$$ 89 $$

PEOPLE notice the care that you give your teeth. Care for your teeth so that they look the best they possibly can.

$$ 90 $$

THE longer you delay doing what is necessary, the more you put your personal credibility at stake.

$$$$$$$$$
Reputation

YOUR reputation is the single most important asset you own. It can single-handedly influence the thoughts and opinions that people have of you and affect their actions *before* you have even met. It can shape the expectations of a person, an organization, a city, or the world.

Your reputation invisibly attracts and repels opportunities every day, whether you are conscious of it or not. Your reputation is perpetuated by persistent behavior or altered by a change in behavior.

Your reputation is a sacred personal asset. It is a powerful legacy that can bring you a future of success.

$$ 91 $$

CONSISTENTLY deliver more than you get paid for, and your reputation will bring you more business.

$$ 92 $$

YOUR reputation will ultimately become your greatest legacy and may influence generations to come.

$$ 93 $$

THERE is no advertisement as powerful as a positive reputation traveling fast.

$$ 94 $$

IF your reputation is that you subscribe to the "status quo," opportunities will avoid you.

$$ 95 $$

ONCE you say something, it can never be taken back.

$$ 96 $$

THE faster your company resolves customer complaints, the less time and money it will spend repairing or defending its reputation.

$$ 97 $$

THE calmer you are, the more business your customers and peers will perceive you have the capacity to handle. The busier you get, the more important it is to remain calm.

$$ 98 $$

YOUR reputation and, by extension, your endorsement are the two most important business assets you have. Your reputation becomes transferable when you endorse someone else.

46

$$ 99 $$

NEVER make negative comments or spread rumors about anyone. It depreciates their reputation *and yours.*

$$ 100 $$

THE only way to keep a good reputation is to continuously earn it.

$$ 101 $$

IF your reputation were worn on your face, would it give you the credibility you need for success?

$$ 102 $$

If you want to see how powerful a reputation is, write down the reputations of several people you know personally. It will become clear why people either are attracted to them or avoid them.

$$ 103 $$

People will take extraordinary action based on another person's reputation. They will leave their jobs, voluntarily work for another, sell their stock, change their outlook—all based on the reputation an authority figure has earned.

$$ 104 $$

You can never accurately judge a person's character until you observe their actions while under emotional pressure.

$$ 105 $$

Take care of your suppliers. They are your "source line" and speak to everyone in your industry.

$$ 106 $$

A poor reputation can bring a company to bankruptcy, and a good one can bring it repeat sales without advertising.

$$ 107 $$

ON the basis of reputation alone, people will pay far more for a brand item than the exact same generic one.

$$ 108 $$

AN organization builds its reputation by consistently offering excellent products and services, demonstrating sensitivity to employees' needs, and also by contributing a portion of its resources back to society.

$$ 109 $$

A STRONG reputation leads to authority and influence. Authority and influence are the foundation of power.

$$ 110 $$

THE degree to which people will be inclined to present opportunities to you is often proportionate to the reputation that precedes you.

$$ 111 $$

You risk your own reputation when you surround yourself with people whose reputations are at a lower standard than yours.

$$ 112 $$

ONE way to evaluate your own reputation is to think about what would be said of you at your eulogy.

$$ 113 $$

IF you are spending time defending your reputation, you have problems.

$$ 114 $$

TO rebuild your reputation, it is often necessary to go back and finish those things you left incomplete.

$$ 115 $$

WHEN business and opportunities are attracted to you and you cannot identify their source, it is your reputation at work.

$$ 116 $$

YOUR reputation can and will travel faster than you.

$$ 117 $$

A COMPANY's good reputation builds consumer confidence and trust *before* the purchase is made.

That's why companies with a solid reputation can charge more than their competitors.

$$ 118 $$

YOUR reputation can take years to build, yet can take only seconds to destroy. Restoring a damaged reputation can take as long or longer than it did to build it in the first place; in many cases, the damage may be permanent.

$$ 119 $$

THE moment you blame, you are depreciating your reputation. The moment you accept responsiblity, you are appreciating your reputation.

$$ 120 $$

To find out how much the reputation of a company is worth, compute the value of "goodwill." Many companies' most valuable asset is their goodwill.

$$$$$$$$$ Negotiation

NEARLY everything in business contains a component of negotiation. The more skilled you are at negotiating, the more often you will get what you want. Skilled negotiators are people who carefully weigh and evaluate the outcome of their communication in advance. They are particularly conscious of how their communications will be interpreted on the other side of the table, carefully shaping their questions or actions to bring about the desired response.

Skilled negotiators have acquired an instinct for knowing when to move forward and when to retreat. They know when to leverage time, information, finances, and concerns. They are particularly sensitive to making sure that the other side feels that they are winning in the negotiation, too. They are skilled in being able to enroll you in their point of view and gain agreement.

Here are some tools to increase the effectiveness of your negotiations.

$$ 121 $$

WHEN negotiating, always listen to the other person's point of view and interests first. He or she may be willing to give you more than you expected.

$$ 122 $$

NEVER make a proposal—written or verbal— until you have complete clarity about what the other person wants and why. This knowledge will vastly increase the effectiveness of your proposals and lead to an increase in your income.

$$ 123 $$

OFTEN, the easiest way to move a negotiation forward is to remove some of the risk for the other party.

$$ 124 $$

NEVER compromise what you want before the negotiations start. Ask for at least 100 percent of what you want without estimating or assuming what will be acceptable to the other party. You can always negotiate any difference later.

$$ 125 $$

WHEN negotiating, there are usually more issues at stake than money alone; for example, control, pride, security, health insurance, pension, duties, a child's future, taxes, options, responsibilities, terms, selected assets, market changes, stock, warrants, rights, and interest can all be valuable negotiation factors. You negotiate effectively and win the most once you are aware of all of the issues at stake.

$$ 126 $$

THE best way to make a good deal is to have the ability to walk away from it.

$$ 127 $$

THE best time to ask for a raise is when you are given additional responsibilities.

$$ 128 $$

THE best time to assign additional responsibilities is when you give a raise.

$$ 129 $$

WHEN negotiating, the side with the most facts and information has a tremendous advantage. Information is the currency of an effective negotiator.

Always acquire all of the facts and information you need first. Preparation pays.

$$ 130 $$

LOOKING beyond your personal and business resources can often reveal a strategic alliance with a competitor or supplier, which can strengthen your negotiating position.

$$ 131 $$

WHEN negotiating, it is often easier to ask for more and take less than it is to take less and return later to ask for more.

$$ 132 $$

WHEN you know *all* of the obstacles, you are in a much better negotiating position than if you successfully address a few obstacles, only to find out later that more obstacles exist. The best way to find out what all the potential obstacles are is to ask.

$$ 133 $$

FEAR always distorts logic.

$$ 134 $$

BRING a certified check made out for 10 percent less than you are willing to spend. You may be surprised at how many times you will leave with what you want.

$$ 135 $$

REMEMBER, it is almost always easier to buy than it is to sell. Therefore, the buyer has more leverage in most negotiations, even when it doesn't necessarily appear that way.

$$ 136 $$

IF you are paying cash, always negotiate a lower price. The seller immediately incurs less cost to sell to you, since he or she has no credit card transaction costs, no bad debt or collection costs, and no waiting time to be paid.

$$ 137 $$

IF you cannot get a lower price paying cash, then pay with a credit card. Besides being able to pay later for something you can begin benefiting from today, you can gain valuable (credit card) airline mileage credits or discounts, which you may be able to sell or use later, effectively reducing the price you paid.

$$ 138 $$

IF you are negotiating for construction of a new home, or for the purchase of a boat, car, or any other big-ticket item, you will usually pay less if you "package" all of the items you want included and *then* negotiate the price, rather than negotiating separately for each item.

$$ 139 $$

Iᴛ is important to note that in any negotiation, the issues less meaningful to you might be the ones most meaningful to the other party. Never reveal what is most important to you at the start. This way you can give in on the little things and gain the big ones that matter most to you.

$$ 140 $$

Eᴠᴇʀʏᴛʜɪɴɢ is negotiable—in any transaction, and in any business—from government to big department stores to the local supermarket.

$$ 141 $$

CONSIDER negotiating more strategic alliances with your suppliers, customers, and/or your competitors. By identifying and working with each other's core competencies, new levels of efficiency can be reached and more profits generated than were individually attainable.

$$ 142 $$

IT is far better to negotiate face-to-face than over a telephone or through the mail. By being in front of the person, you have the advantage of observing body language and facial expressions, which are often far more telling than words alone.

$$ 143 $$

IF you are unwilling to negotiate with your customers, someone else will.

$$ 144 $$

THE best person to have at your negotiations is someone who already has an unbiased relationship with all of the parties. This person has the trust that is necessary to resolve any differences and can expedite any negotiation.

$$ 145 $$

MOST decisions in a negotiation are made emotionally and rationalized later.

$$ 146 $$

WHEN negotiating transactions that involve an ongoing relationship, it is important to make sure that both sides benefit from the transaction. Otherwise, you will have negotiated a temporary solution to a long-term problem.

$$ 147 $$

DURING a negotiation, it would be wise not to take anything personally. If you leave personalities out of it, you will be able to see opportunities more objectively.

$$ 148 $$

THE more emotionally invested a party is in the success of the negotiation, the tougher it will be for that party to walk away.

$$ 149 $$

IF you are negotiating with a public company, first obtain a copy of its quarterly report and other information that is available on the Internet. This detailed information on the company's business can help you gain a valuable advantage in your negotiation.

$$ 150 $$

THE more logic and analysis play a role in your negotiations, the longer your negotiations will take. Negotiations will move more rapidly if you can create compelling reasons for the other side to act now.

$$ 151 $$

THE more options the other side believes you have, the more leverage you will gain in your negotiations.

$$$$$$$$ Listening

THE ability to communicate effectively with others is your single most important skill. It is directly related to your ability to produce consistent results. Communication is composed of both speaking and listening. Speaking is a matter of tonality, phrasing, pausing, and drama. Although we often prize these speaking skills, we frequently neglect to develop our ability to listen.

Listening is a matter of hearing a communication, detached from the filters of our beliefs, judgments, and assessments. When actively practiced, listening enables us to hear and validate someone else, without his or her communication being filtered by our own internal dialogue or agenda. This results in deeper comprehension between the listener and the speaker. It is through this deeper comprehension that formerly unheard possibilities—and thus, opportunities—unfold.

$$ 152 $$

You will always learn more by listening than by speaking.

$$ 153 $$

Oftentimes, people will not say what they mean. Always listen to a person's commitment behind what he or she is saying. Therein lies the truth in that person's communication.

$$ 154 $$

RECORD your conversations. During playback, ask yourself if you would buy from you.

$$ 155 $$

MOST people need and want someone who will listen to them with undivided attention.

$$ 156 $$

YOUR hearing can be fine-tuned to listen for anything. For example, I often listen for "opportunity." Try it and you'll be surprised by how much more of it you will hear! With my employees, I listen for where I can "acknowledge them." With my clients, I listen for where I can make the "biggest difference" for them. What do you actively listen for?

$$ 157 $$

IF you spend more time asking appropriate questions rather than giving answers or opinions, your listening skills will increase.

$$ 158 $$

IF you ask potential buyers of your service "What do you see as the specific benefits of working with us?" they will often communicate enough reasons to sell themselves.

$$ 159 $$

SHOWING people you sincerely care about them can often be as easy as listening to them.

$$ 160 $$

To encounter less resistance when communicating, consider changing your mode of communication. For example, some people respond better to verbal communication, while others respond better to written communication. Try it. You may be pleasantly surprised at how much more receptive they are to you.

$$ 161 $$

RESPONDING to what is happening is often more effective than reacting to it. Reacting includes an emotional component that will often impair your ability to listen and cause a loss of objectivity.

$$ 162 $$

THE only people worthy of hearing your goals are the people who will be genuinely supportive and help you to achieve them.

$$ 163 $$

IT's a good idea to discover your customer's needs before you explain why you have the right product or service for him or her. Listening first often provides the key to closing the sale.

$$ 164 $$

INDIVIDUAL and team performance will have more velocity when the organization's culture provides for straight, honest speaking, listening, and debate.

$$ 165 $$

OPPORTUNITIES are everywhere. Listen first, before speaking, and you will hone your personal radar.

$$ 166 $$

NEVER interrupt another person who is speaking. It is insulting, discourteous, and disrespectful, all of which will cost you in the long run.

$$ 167 $$

BEGINNING any correspondence with "As you may already know," or "As you know," or "As you have undoubtedly already heard," places you at a high risk of insulting readers in the event that they do not already know or haven't heard.

$$ 168 $$

BEGIN practicing your listening skills much like an artist would practice a brush stroke. When you take listening to the level of an art form, your ability to hear things that other people don't will increase . . . and so will your opportunities.

$$ 169 $$

ALWAYS listen to people as if they are speaking 100 percent truthfully. Whether you agree or not, most people will speak what is true from their standpoint of reality.

$$ 170 $$

LISTEN 85 percent of the time; speak 15 percent. Your whole world will shift, and you will learn more, too. People value a good listener.

$$ 171 $$

MOST of the listening we do is rather selfish. We listen to our internal dialogue more than we listen to others. You can shift your internal dialogue and become a more effective listener by immersing yourself in daily positive input from positive people, CDs, and books.

Fill your mind with positive "Millionaire Thoughts." Download the free 365 Ways to Become a Millionaire screen saver for your computer moni-

tor at home and at work. Visit www.365WaystoBec
omeaMillionaire.com.

$$ 172 $$

B(Y deliberately paying attention to the details of
a conversation, you will be validating the person
speaking and will increase your own effectiveness.

$$ 173 $$

P(EOPLE will feel safer around you and speak
truthfully to you when they feel you are listening
intently to them.

$$ 174 $$

WHEN people hear the truth, it will usually quiet their internal dialogue and allow them to learn at a faster pace. The truth, once heard, can triumph over confusion, and can cause more effective action.

$$ 175 $$

ARROGANCE is listening to your internal dialogue rather than the communication of another.

$$ 176 $$

LISTENING can provide a perspective as powerful as seeing. It can often provide a window for opportunities and actions that otherwise would be missed.

$$ 177 $$

WHEN you rearrange the letters *l i s t e n*, what word do you get? *Silent*.

$$ 178 $$

THE best people to listen to are those who have already been successful accomplishing exactly what you are seeking to accomplish.

$$ 179 $$

LISTEN to people who attract and earn substantially more money than you do. People who attract and earn more money are often a stimulus and an inspiration for others.

$$ 180 $$

WHAT you like, what you want, and what you wish for are not as interesting to people as what you are doing about it.

$$ 181 $$

IF you listen carefully, you will hear that most people are crying out for love.

$$$$$$$$ Entrepreneurialism

THE entrepreneurial spirit has developed a charismatic mystique in American society and indeed in much of the world. Exactly what is the spirit that has become such an important part of our cultural fabric? To define the entrepreneurial spirit, one must first define the entrepreneur—the person who embodies that energy. The entrepreneur is a broker of an ever-changing portfolio of products and ideas who displays a range of possibilities that entices people. He or she has gone beyond the traditional paradigm of employment into one that is much grander and more exciting. The entrepreneur is a person who takes risks and is involved directly with the art and process of creating—out of nothing—something valuable to someone else. The entrepreneur has become the "rainmaker" in corporate America—and in government—and is currently transforming the economies of the world.

$$ 182 $$

THE entrepreneur has turned his or her personal radar to a frequency that specifically looks and listens for opportunities. Opportunities are everywhere when you are tuned into this frequency.

$$ 183 $$

FORGET the lottery. Bet on yourself instead.

$$ 184 $$

IF you are bigger than your mistakes and failures, you will recover quickly and move forward. If you are paralyzed by your mistakes and failures, then you need to become more aware of your uniqueness and value. The faster you emotionally detach yourself from your mistakes and failures, the more spontaneously you will be able to generate new opportunities and results.

$$ 185 $$

MASTERING your work includes mastering the ability to replace yourself. This frees you up for greater opportunities and self-fulfillment.

$$ 186 $$

THE bigger your purpose, the more vitality you will have at the end of the day.

$$ 187 $$

THE longer you are stuck in analysis of any opportunity or situation, the more reasons you will find to hold back, delay, and inadvertently risk the loss of the opportunity itself.

$$ 188 $$

DON'T go into business solely to produce a good profit. Produce a good product or service, and when it is combined with your entrepreneurial skills, the outcome will be profit.

$$ 189 $$

CONFIDENCE and certainty will get you further than anything else will.

$$ 190 $$

THE more of the customer's risk you take out of your products and services, the more easily you will increase your sales.

$$ 191 $$

THE more complexity you take out of your products and services, the faster you will make your sales.

$$ 192 $$

THE fastest way for you to attract more opportunity in your company is to consistently outperform expectations.

$$ 193 $$

ENTREPRENEURS have developed a skill for rising above their circumstances rather than being suppressed or stopped by them. Because their results are unrelated to their circumstances, circumstances are never held responsible or blamed for their results.

$$ 194 $$

Use your free time for self-development. Listen to motivational or educational CDs while driving to work. Read an inspirational book before bed. Always nourish your brain cells with positive input. Start today!

Visit 365WaystoBecomeaMillionaire.com and download daily positive "Millionaire Thoughts"!

$$ 195 $$

BE willing to trust your instincts, especially if you cannot find answers elsewhere.

$$ 196 $$

BE anchored to some ideal, philosophy, or cause that keeps you too excited to sleep.

$$ 197 $$

WHEN planning the future of your company, always look to see how you would reinvent it if you started over from nothing. Then you will be able to act in a way that is in concert with where it needs to go rather than where it is right now.

$$ 198 $$

CRITICISM can be a double-edged sword. For some people, it can provide the fuel necessary to take effective action, yet for others, it may suppress creativity and their willingness to take risks. The entrepreneur is conscious of the effect his or her criticism has upon others.

$$ 199 $$

OFTENTIMES, money alone will not motivate people. What would motivate people more than money? Time off, equity, security (such as health insurance, retirement plan, etc.), being part of a team, contributing to a cause, recognition, acknowledgment, or a changed perspective of the future.

$$ 200 $$

THE difference between the amateur and the professional is not that the amateur is incapable of producing the same results. It is that the professional can do it consistently time after time, with predictable results.

$$ 201 $$

THE only way to create new operating standards is to challenge current paradigms. This outside-in thinking can often bring greater opportunities than working within existing standards or models.

$$ 202 $$

IF you rely solely on one form or method of marketing your products or services, you are heading for a crisis. *Nothing* works forever.

$$ 203 $$

SATISFIED customers return. Enthusiastic customers return and refer. To make your customers enthusiastic about your products and services, be enthusiastic first. Enthusiasm is contagious.

$$ 204 $$

WHAT distinguishes an entrepreneurial company is its ability to innovate, respond, change, and adapt at an astounding rate.

$$ 205 $$

WHEN an organization is growing rapidly, some people will deselect themselves, usually because the pace is beyond their emotional or physical capacity. Allowing them to leave provides the space necessary to attract and recruit new talent.

$$ 206 $$

To increase your effectiveness, make your emotions subordinate to your commitments.

$$ 207 $$

Always look for the expanding market. It is easier to profit by positioning yourself in front of a mushrooming market than by investing efforts in mature or saturated markets. Go where the expansion is flowing, and you will gain a higher rate of return on your efforts.

$$ 208 $$

YOUR emotional investment in the way things are currently being accomplished is likely to be one of your biggest barriers to change. Change comes easiest when you detach from your personal investment of time, energy, and involvement.

$$ 209 $$

THE vast majority of the population spends a great deal of effort and money protecting themselves from losing what they already have. Highly successful people, however, spend a great deal of money and effort risking what they already have to get what they want.

$$ 210 $$

YOUR personal capacity to handle more valuable projects will go up when you appreciate yourself more and you express gratitude to others.

$$ 211 $$

ALL success comes from a combination of implementation and knowledge. Knowledge alone is meaningless without action.

$$ 212 $$

THE most common cause of insufficient results is insufficient action.

What actions can you take right now to cause an increase in your results?

$$$$$$$$ Money

CORPORATE culture is continuing to shift toward a balance between work and other values, such as family and leisure time. However, money remains the primary source of security, expanded choices, and comfort for most Americans and indeed for much of the world today. This ultimate scorekeeper of success accounts for the motivation of individuals, businesses, and nations throughout the world.

Money is in abundant supply in the United States as businesses continue to develop profit centers based on providing technology, innovation, and talent.

The most significant amount of money will be generated by those companies and individuals who have developed a consciousness for consistently generating value to others combined with a skill for leveraging their technology, innovation, and talent.

$$ 213 $$

THE very first step to building wealth is to spend less than you make.

$$ 214 $$

INVEST 5 to 10 percent of your income every year in your own business training and development. If you work for a company, ask them to subsidize or

pay for your training. If your company is not interested in your self-improvement, leave.

$$ 215 $$

To increase your financial skills, read at least
two well-known financial magazines or newspa-
pers every week. You will become more sophisti-
cated in leveraging your money and having it work
for you while you sleep.

$$ 216 $$

When dealing with your personal accountant,
always remember that you manage him or her.
Never wait for your accountant to manage you.

Never assume that your accountant will tell you something if you fail to ask.

$$ 217 $$

BEING skilled at your work will not necessarily make you more money. Being highly committed to making more money and leveraging your skill is what makes more money.

$$ 218 $$

TO maximize your personal income at your company, find the most profitable division and get a transfer. Find that division's most profitable products or services. Locate the person who sells the most of those products or services or leads that division, and learn as much as that person can teach you as fast as possible. Within months, your income should climb substantially.

$$ 219 $$

PAY your key suppliers in advance. They will usually offer you enticing discounts and provide incentives to maintain your account. You will also have far less paperwork.

$$ 220 $$

INCREASING your personal income per hour or the number of hours you work will usually not earn you as large a personal financial gain as investing your money wisely. Make your money work consistently harder than you do.

$$ 221 $$

AFTER being waited on by another human being, tip until it feels good. It will increase your personal self-worth.

$$ 222 $$

THE more you increase employees' rewards and reduce their risks, the more they will perform. Fear of risk or providing inadequate rewards often causes employee paralysis.

$$ 223 $$

IF you are considering borrowing, it may be easier to focus your energy on increasing your business to generate the money you need rather than taking your focus off your business to go through the borrowing process in the first place.

$$ 224 $$

NEVER lend money to family members, unless you can live without getting it back.

$$ 225 $$

IF you need to borrow, the following may be easier sources of money than your bank: retirement plans, insurance policies, pension plans, credit un-ions, home equity loans, relatives, suppliers, and your customers.

$$ 226 $$

PREPAYMENT for services or payment when ser-vices are rendered is essential to the integrity of your organization. Unlike many products, services have their highest value at the time they are ren-dered. Proof: The longer you wait to collect your money for services you render, the less chance you have of collecting it!

$$ 227 $$

IN the United States, it is easier to buy almost anything than it is to sell it. Make sure you count to ten before buying a house, plane, car, boat, or any other possession that may at some point possess you.

$$ 228 $$

THE cheapest way to finance your business is to have your customers pay in advance for your services or products.

$$ 229 $$

MAKE sure you are being fiscally responsible for your future by investing in a retirement plan. The government may not have the resources to take care of your financial needs later. Moreover, the current tax savings may be too generous to ignore.

$$ 230 $$

THE easier you make it for your customers to pay you, the faster you will get paid. Try any of the following: credit card payment via your website or at a toll-free telephone number; including a postage-paid return-payment envelope; arranging "easy/instant credit" for your customers with a credit card company; electronic check payment or automatic funds transfer; shipping COD; fast-payment discount; early-payment gift; and/or a higher published price for delayed payment.

$$ 231 $$

Make a list of the suppliers who would benefit if your business grows. These are the suppliers who would most likely provide you with the resources you need because they have a direct interest in your company's future. They can provide you with financing, information, technology, and talent that will propel you forward, and they will benefit directly from the growth in business that their resources make possible.

$$ 232 $$

Always maintain credit lines on your personal and business banking accounts. These reserves may provide the instant cash you need to handle a crisis or an immediate opportunity.

$$ 233 $$

IN a personal service business, your fees will usually rise in accordance with your self-esteem and not necessarily in accordance with your level of skill or results.

$$ 234 $$

EVERY year or two, bring your tax returns to another accountant for a second opinion. This fresh analysis will usually be well worth your investment with respect to tax savings and/or valuable tax perspectives gained.

$$ 235 $$

CONTROLLING costs is not as powerful as controlling income. Costs have a finite potential, while income has an infinite potential. Focus your resources on generating more income—there is greater potential there.

$$ 236 $$

ALWAYS communicate promptly with your creditors regarding any inability to make payments on your debts, or they will sue you, and you will have bigger problems to consume your scarce resources.

$$ 237 $$

IF things often seem too expensive, either you are not earning enough income or your standards are too high. It is much easier to increase your income than it is to lower your standards.

$$ 238 $$

YOU will not easily be able to build a financial empire for yourself unless you are willing to help build other people's financial empires. Prosperity attracts prosperity.

$$ 239 $$

THE more people you can positively influence, the higher your earnings.

$$ 240 $$

BEAR in mind that it is always easier to lend money than it is to get it back.

$$ 241 $$

DON'T lend money unless it is 100 percent secured with the borrower's assets, and the borrower pays for any and all necessary collections for late payments or default(s). And then lend it only if you receive a percentage of the profit from the venture your loan makes possible.

$$ 242 $$

MAKE a list of your core competencies—those things you are best at. Maximizing your activities around your core competencies and delegating everything else will assure you greater earnings.

$$ 243 $$

IF you believe that wealth is attracted to you, you will attract more opportunities and money. You must be mentally prepared to be wealthy or your wealth will be temporary at best.

$$$$$$$$
Productivity

Historically, business increased productivity by implementing new efficiencies or by managing capacities. Both personal and business productivity gains used to be limited to the physical universe. However, as our economy has become redefined by its technology and talent, the paradigm of efficiency and productivity has shifted from the quantity of physical products we produce to the quality of the interactions we have. The velocity with which productivity gains can be realized has become directly related to the degree that human interactions can be made more effective.

To make remarkable gains in productivity, an organization must be committed to removing disharmony among its employees while at the same time generating an environment of cooperation, accountability, and urgency.

$$ 244 $$

For your business model to be productive, your customers' emotional needs must be fulfilled by your products or services, or your customers will go elsewhere.

$$ 245 $$

Always delegate projects to people who can do them well. Otherwise, the people who you have delegated to will feel defeated and adopt a lower sense of self-esteem, which will decrease their productivity.

$$ 246 $$

To increase your personal productivity, make a list of all your strengths. Maximize your actions that use these strengths, and delegate your weaknesses to someone for whom they are strengths.

$$ 247 $$

ALWAYS focus on your primary objective, not the barriers or circumstances that appear to be in your way. A high level of conviction will break through any barriers or circumstances and increase your productivity.

119

$$ 248 $$

A SERVICE business will be more limited by the emotional capacity of its staff and owners than by any other single factor. To increase productivity, remove dysfunction.

$$ 249 $$

THE more productive your staff is, the higher their morale will be. If morale is low, do everything to boost productivity, and staff morale will increase. If morale is consistently low, you may be over-staffed and/or need to communicate your vision more effectively.

$$ 250 $$

MAKE a list of all the unfinished and half-finished projects that are burdening you. Responsibly completing them, delegating them, or eliminating them will make your phone ring with additional opportunities. Burdens slow you down and slow down your business cycle.

$$ 251 $$

MEASURE every individual and/or group activity that adds value for your customers. Providing incentives that are based on setting benchmarks in these key areas of activity will increase productivity.

$$ 252 $$

Sugar and caffeine are short-term stimulants that rob your body of long-term energy and productivity.

$$ 253 $$

Salaried employees can easily become complacent. You can generate more productivity and higher self-esteem for your employees by providing performance-based pay and incentives.

$$ 254 $$

People who are passionately committed to their work will usually go beyond what is comfortable and produce at higher levels. People become passionately committed when they have a purpose bigger than themselves.

$$ 255 $$

As new portable technologies become available, bring them into your car, home, and elsewhere. This investment will allow you to become more productive with time that would otherwise be spent passively.

$$ 256 $$

IT is always more productive to address any conflict sooner rather than later. Conflicts have a way of escalating unless they are diffused quickly.

$$ 257 $$

STUDIES show that people are more productive before lunch than after. Why not make lunch hour one hour later or start business hours one hour earlier? 8 to 1 anyone?

$$ 258 $$

IN competitive businesses, a backlog of work will slow down your ability to increase sales. In a noncompetitive industry, a backlog will entice new competitors.

$$ 259 $$

BEING busy and being productive are not necessarily related.

$$ 260 $$

THE fastest way to change results is to change the people producing them.

$$ 261 $$

IF you make the assignments and tasks you delegate to others too complicated, you will slow up their process and results. Emphasize the overall importance while minimizing detailed explanations and projects will get completed faster.

$$ 262 $$

I⊤ may be more productive to illustrate your points rather than be limited to words alone. People think in pictures, and a picture can say a thousand words.

$$ 263 $$

A⌊ᴡᴀʏꜱ travel with the technology needed to retrieve your e-mail, send faxes, and print documents. This will increase your efficiency, response time, and productivity.

$$ 264 $$

IN marketing, preemptive efforts are usually much more productive and profitable than reactive efforts.

$$ 265 $$

WHEN employees have something personally at stake, their productivity will increase.

$$ 266 $$

THERE is a natural flow to life. If you are encountering too much resistance in your endeavor, you may want to step back to gain a new perspective, or ask for help.

$$ 267 $$

A⊤ least once a year, consult technology experts who can reduce paper consumption, provide technological solutions to increase efficiencies, and address anything else that can speed up production. Proper utilization and application of new technology will keep you more productive than your competitors, while failure to upgrade will quickly erode your profit margins and your ability to compete effectively.

$$ 268 $$

W<small>HEN</small> the cost of your sales is persistently rising, it may be more productive to use your resources to buy your competitors. Often, you can purchase market share, distribution channels, facilities, talent, and/or technology faster and at less cost than developing it yourself.

$$ 269 $$

T<small>HE</small> best place to use big words is in a crossword puzzle. Big words are frequently misunderstood and will reduce your productivity.

$$ 270 $$

IF you want a list of all the bottlenecks or capacity blocks in your organization, have your staff make a list of everything they least like to do.

$$ 271 $$

HIRING more competent people to do the work is more productive in the long run, because it inevitably frees you up to generate more results. If you hire less competent people, you may save a few dollars initially, but you will certainly spend more time cleaning up the messes or doing the work yourself.

$$ 272 $$

Aɴʏ company can save paper, time, money, and labor by electronically invoicing the customer and by obtaining authorization for automatic electronic deductions from a credit card or bank account. Offer your customers incentives to switch to electronic payment of your invoices. You will be paid faster and operate more efficiently. So will your customer.

$$ 273 $$

Rᴇᴍᴇᴍʙᴇʀ to regularly nurture yourself. You cannot sustain or increase your productivity without replenishing yourself. Otherwise, you will run on empty and your productivity will suffer.

$$$$$$$$ Time

WHAT is man-made, a complete illusion, self-liquidating, and has more value than money? The answer is *time*. In spite of grandma's age-old recipe, time no longer equals money. Money is available in abundant supply; time is not. Companies with no value or that didn't exist yesterday have billions (yes, *billions*) in valuations overnight. Time has lost its relationship to money and results.

Broad access to the Internet and other technological wonders has enabled us to transcend time. We can travel through cyberspace and instantaneously visit sites around the globe. Cyberspace allows us to be seen and heard at multiple locations around the world through real-time networks. A keystroke or click of a mouse can now accomplish great feats for work or pleasure on the order of what the invention of the lightbulb did for darkness or the automobile did for travel. Health care technology has also enabled us to transcend time. Our life span is increasing to the point where we can expect to live to see multiple generations of our descendants. Considering the rapid breakthroughs in biogenetic research, it may soon be possible to live long enough to attend our grandchildren's hundredth birthday party.

Because we can transcend time and expect to live longer, it would seem that we have all the time in the world. The downside to having the world at our fingertips, however, is that the faster technology enables us to accomplish our goals, the more goals there are to accomplish. The instant society is here, and it is here *now*. As technology increasingly penetrates our lives and the value of a balanced life takes precedence over money, time has become the ultimate scarce resource of individuals and corporations.

$$ 274 $$

To be complacent is to disrespect the most valuable and irreplaceable commodity—time—and carries the largest potential risks to anyone or any company.

$$ 275 $$

THE more assessments, judgments, and evaluations you have, the more time you will be stalled. People who accept responsibility and reach the top fastest tend to be less judgmental and don't over-analyze situations.

$$ 276 $$

Most people connect their results with the amount of time they have invested. If you change your thinking to "results have no relationship to time," this new perspective will give rise to previously unforeseen possibilities.

$$ 277 $$

The more your presentation appeals to your prospect's logic, the longer your prospect will take to decide, and the longer it will take to make the sale.

$$ 278 $$

You must be able to quickly detach from your emotional investment in any personal failures, setbacks, or disappointments. The freedom to move forward to new opportunities and to produce results comes from living in the present, not the past.

$$ 279 $$

Spending more time and/or more effort is a finite game of getting results. Changing your thinking and perspectives is an infinite game and is therefore more worthy of your attention and resources.

$$ 280 $$

ALWAYS delegate activities that require less expertise than you have. This will free up your time to notice and take action on opportunities that otherwise may pass you by.

$$ 281 $$

TRACK every moment of your twenty-four-hour day and then see what activities produce the greatest outcome or profit. Delegate all other activities to someone else who has the expertise, or else hire the expertise you need. Do it now.

$$ 282 $$

Do not waste your precious time being occupied with what you think other people are thinking. Not only is it an ineffective use of your time, it will also result in misguided assumptions.

$$ 283 $$

No individual or company can grow beyond its ability to stay organized. A lack of organization is disrespect for time.

$$ 284 $$

If you and your organization are not providing "instant," "now," "on-the-spot," immediate-response service, you are sending your customers to your competitors.

$$ 285 $$

To save time, be vigilant about eliminating any process or system that does not add consumer value to your product or service. The best way to know what does not add value is to ask.

$$ 286 $$

If you procrastinate implementing an idea long enough, someone else will inevitably innovate the same idea and run with it. Procrastination is one of the most costly personal and business expenses.

$$ 287 $$

FOR most busy executives, an effective electronic PDA or manual time-management planner is an essential tool. If you are working without one, you would increase your available time with one.

$$ 288 $$

MAKE a habit of having a place for everything and putting everything in its place. You will spend less time unnecessarily looking for things.

$$ 289 $$

MAKE a list of everything that is holding you back. Then handle each task or issue one at a time until you are free.

$$ 290 $$

THE more your time is consumed by responding to problems, the less ability you will have to focus your resources on generating opportunities. Resolve problems quickly and to completion. Automate your response systems so that in the future, the same problems will be answered seamlessly, without the recurring attention of valuable human resources.

$$ 291 $$

IF you nurture your mind, body, and spirit, your time will expand. You will gain a new perspective that will allow you to accomplish much more.

$$ 292 $$

As your time becomes more valuable, make sure to invest in and upgrade to more efficient systems and technologies.

$$ 293 $$

REFRESH your business and personal phone list annually. It will take less time to sort through it in the future.

$$ 294 $$

Be willing to let go of the old in order to create something new. Regularly upgrade your clothing, automobiles, and your own personal packaging. It will keep you alive, vibrant, and growing.

$$ 295 $$

Reassign the time you spend watching television to reading a trade or computer magazine. You will expand your knowledge, be more effective at your work, and learn about additional opportunities for increased results with fewer efforts.

$$ 296 $$

IF your mind is occupied or cluttered, your senses will be suppressed, and you would be better off making decisions at another time. Clarity of mind and access to your innate senses always come without effort and provide your best decisions.

$$ 297 $$

WAITING in line, getting a busy signal, being put on hold, or plodding through a slow or cumbersome website are all time wasters that will annoy the majority of people and cause many to go elsewhere for a faster response to their wants and needs.

$$ 298 $$

Consider completely restructuring your work (or your entire company) for maximum productivity. One of the most effective executives I know sends information he is working on over the Internet to a company located halfway around the world, where they work on his projects while he sleeps. The next day, his projects are several steps closer to completion and ready for his attention.

$$ 299 $$

Most people schedule appointments and meetings that have a specific start time with little emphasis on an "end" time. Therefore, the time allotted is frequently expanded and unnecessarily wasted.

An improved respect for your time would include a specifically stated time to begin and *end* each meeting.

$$ 300 $$

HAVE a written agenda in advance of every meeting. If there isn't one, request it or provide it. The productivity and time-effectiveness of your meetings will increase exponentially.

$$ 301 $$

WHEN your business is more important than your family or taking care of yourself, you are not delegating enough.

$$ 302 $$

THE projects you focus on will gain momentum. Distractions will always lessen momentum and results from any given project. Permitting distractions shows disrespect for your time.

$$ 303 $$

ALWAYS subscribe to the fastest broadband Internet connection available to you. In the long run, it will save you time and money. Always work on multiple computer monitors—that will save you time and money too.

$$ 304 $$

To maximize your time, carry a handheld recorder and dictate your thoughts each day; otherwise, some of your best ideas will be lost. P.S.: I dictated this entire book on a handheld recorder while walking to work over the course of a summer.

$$$$$$$$
Confrontation

WE usually restrict our use of the word "confrontation" to situations in which we communicate what are often difficult truths to others. But the most difficult person to confront with the truth is ourselves. Highly successful people know that they cannot confront anything outside of themselves without simultaneously confronting what is inside of themselves. Self-confrontation provides us with new levels of vitality, freedom, and clarity of purpose.

While most people will make extraordinary efforts to modify their behavior to avoid confrontation, highly effective people actively invite feedback and coaching on their behavior and performance. Rather than experiencing confrontation as a cause for upset, they see it as a means of transformation. For example, confrontation has become part of the environment in some corporate cultures that allows them to channel their energy more appropriately to where it will create the most value. The essence of confrontation is uncovering the truth. In doing so, new perspectives are born, giving access to results that may have been previously unforeseen.

When we interpret confrontation as a contribution, it becomes welcome. When we interpret it as an attack, we feel the need for protective defenses and maneuvers. Highly effective people will always see confrontation as the former. To become more effective, we must embrace the fruits of confrontation rather than act to avoid the potential discomfort.

$$ 305 $$

IF you complain or acknowledge anything lacking in your life, you reinforce the lack. Confront this negative habit by regularly acknowledging what you have. It will increase your personal velocity.

$$ 306 $$

TAKING things personally will distort your ability to respond effectively.

$$ 307 $$

THE most difficult person to confront is yourself. However, once you confront an issue within yourself, the issue will evaporate, leaving in its place a new experience of freedom.

$$ 308 $$

As long as you see problems as existing outside of yourself, you will be out of control. If you see all problems as originating within yourself, it will be much easier to confront and overcome the problems. You will also complain less.

$$ 309 $$

If you stand for something bigger than yourself, it will be easier to get yourself out of the way.

$$ 310 $$

THE most effective person to point your finger at is you. Accepting responsibility for your actions and inaction—without wasting time on criticizing yourself—is the hallmark of an effective person.

$$ 311 $$

ONE of the most difficult things any employer must confront is firing an employee. Oftentimes, however, you are freeing this person up to find employment where he or she can experience greater personal fulfillment and growth.

$$ 312 $$

IF you are in doubt as to whether there is anything you have been unwilling to confront, make a list of all the things, conversations, people, and actions you have been avoiding.

$$ 313 $$

MOST people are willing to stay in relationships that do not support them out of concern for confronting an uncertain future. Most highly effective people are willing to move on, thus freeing themselves up for new possibilities.

$$ 314 $$

FEAR of confrontation will often cause paralysis. To experience freedom, confront sooner rather than later. If you are stuck, ask for help.

$$ 315 $$

COMPETENT people produce results. When people make excuses, they are covering up their underlying incompetence. Incompetence will ultimately be their downfall unless they are effectively confronted about acquiring the necessary skills.

$$ 316 $$

CONFRONTING a crisis moves people into higher levels of action and creativity. A crisis can be an important tool in many companies to unlock human potential and to accelerate results.

$$ 317 $$

PEOPLE who are willing to be unreasonable and unrealistic, and take actions beyond their comfort levels will always advance more quickly than those who "play it safe" or work the "status quo."

$$ 318 $$

FORGET about what you did yesterday. Your employer is more interested in what you will do today and tomorrow.

$$ 319 $$

IF your results consistently fall short of your desires, you must confront the common denominator: YOU. Results can only consistently improve as much as you do.

$$ 320 $$

SKILLFUL confronting does not leave another person upset. It is not skillful for one person to be made right and another made wrong. Responsible confrontation respects the dignity and position of the other person. When the truth is presented, the listening matches the speaking, and there will be silence.

$$ 321 $$

PEOPLE with reasons and excuses are generally more committed to the "status quo" and failure than they are to success. People who are committed to success rarely have excuses.

$$ 322 $$

THE biggest untapped potential in most organizations is their employees. If you confront the "status quo" and provide rewards that encourage performance and risk, you will have greater innovation, productivity, and excitement in your company.

$$ 323 $$

MANY people avoid confronting others because they fear that others won't like them. Being liked by others is important, but being able to confront and still be liked is a more effective formula for success.

$$ 324 $$

THE fastest way to motivate people to confront their procrastinated projects at work is to increase their accountability while providing personal benefits and/or losses based on their results.

$$ 325 $$

AN employee who is tolerated by an employer is an employee who is requesting to be permanently freed from his or her duties by an employer who is avoiding the inevitable confrontation.

$$ 326 $$

ONE of the toughest things to confront in any company is changing a culture of mediocrity. This is often left for confrontation through a crisis or bankruptcy. The greatest risk for any company is to leave the status quo unchallenged.

$$ 327 $$

MEDIOCRITY will prevail until confronted.

$$ 328 $$

ONE way to view confrontation is to be grateful that someone else thought you were important enough for them to take their time and effort to tell you what is true for them.

$$ 329 $$

THE most powerful thing to confront anyone with is the truth. Successful people not only are able to tell others the truth but also can accomplish this skillfully, leaving the other person grateful.

$$ 330 $$

THE degree to which you avoid confronting something or someone is the degree to which you have allowed that person or thing to have power over you.

$$ 331 $$

If you are constantly confronting the people around you, consider the possibility that your own behavior might be triggering what you find offensive in theirs. Oftentimes by confronting your own behavior, you will automatically shift everyone else's. Try it, you may be surprised!

$$ 332 $$

Your ability to responsibly confront people is one of the key ingredients to getting ahead.

$$ 333 $$

CIRCUMSTANCES are not a valid excuse for a lack of performance. If you cannot confront and overcome your circumstances, your performance will suffer.

$$ 334 $$

FEAR of confrontation can cause paralysis. Most people will go through elaborate mental gymnastics and maneuvers to avoid an inevitable confrontation. Highly effective people, however, will confront as soon as possible to maintain momentum and avoid worrying.

$$$$$$$$$
Leadership

As cultural and economic barriers to trade diminish, the call for effective leadership in organizations and nations has never been greater.

The new leaders will be able to communicate and respond effectively to the diverse needs of this growing culture and global economy. They will be able to merge individuals and groups with a variety of needs and perspectives toward a consensus and common cause. They will communicate a future that inspires effective action and results.

For those who lead, there has never been a time so exciting or one that offers such a vast array of local and global challenges. Leadership is a dance with life itself, challenging even the most competent to transcend differences and communicate in a frictionless manner that relates, informs, and inspires diverse groups of people to effective action.

$$ 335 $$

THE role of an effective leader is to continually create and communicate the company's vision and define the business it is in. It is also to inspire its executives, managers, and staff to effective action.

$$ 336 $$

LEADERS must be conscious of their power to instantly transmit their moods and attitudes to their organizations. Negative moods and attitudes will cause a subtle shift in the productivity of your company. While this may only take moments to ignite, it can be quite costly and time consuming to diffuse.

$$ 337 $$

THE common denominator of all effective leaders is self-discipline.

$$ 338 $$

LEADERS trust and believe in their instincts because they are frequently providing a vision of a future that doesn't yet exist.

$$ 339 $$

LEADERS move their organizations forward with urgency because they know that in the absence of urgency they face extinction.

$$ 340 $$

THE beginning of the end of any business is failing to deliver on what was promised. First, your customers lose faith, and shortly thereafter, your employees lose faith. To make a turnaround, to revitalize productivity and results, leadership must communicate new commitments backed by specific, visible actions—fast.

$$ 341 $$

LEADERS are able to establish an informal network to find necessary information fast. If you can't find information as rapidly as you need it, your ability to lead will be diminished.

$$ 342 $$

EFFECTIVE leaders have an uncanny ability to quickly turn problems into opportunities.

$$ 343 $$

MUSICAL bands and all sports teams always play better when the leader shows up. The same is true for your employees.

$$ 344 $$

WHEN your organization, division, or department stops producing profits over a lengthy time period, you need to increase innovation, communicate a new vision backed by specific actions, or make a major change in staff. If present leadership cannot accomplish this, change leaders.

$$ 345 $$

EFFECTIVE leaders are rarely defensive. Usually, they have taken a stand that does not require them to defend their position but instead encourages others to participate in sharing it with them.

$$ 346 $$

Most people have far greater ability than they will ever use. The purpose of leadership is to inspire this ordinarily untapped human potential to effective action.

$$ 347 $$

The purpose of budgets is to determine what is predictable and make provisions for it. The purpose of effective leadership is to make unpredictable results occur within those budgets.

$$ 348 $$

ORGANIZED, voluntarily committed action is the ideal state of corporate culture. Inspiring these actions with a common vision that defines the business and provides maximum value to its employees, customers, and shareholders is the ideal state of effective leadership.

$$ 349 $$

YOU will lose personal power in the present without a clear vision for the future.

$$ 350 $$

Leaders generally hold themselves to higher standards than others do. They never hedge their communications with words like "try," "attempt," "maybe," or "hopefully." They provide certainty that inspires others to believe in them.

$$ 351 $$

All great leaders have developed their people skills to an intuitive level, whereby they are able to bring out the potential in others. People skills begin with being able to quickly generate credibility and affinity with others.

$$ 352 $$

LEADERSHIP that is driven by ego will not realize the same potential for developing opportunities as leadership driven by a cause or purpose that is greater than self.

$$ 353 $$

IF employees are feeling drained, leaders need to provide a bigger vision. My advice: Leaders could spend more time communicating their vision for their company and the contribution their products and services are making to the world.

$$ 354 $$

IF you are not communicating the vision for your organization, unit, or department, who is?

$$ 355 $$

WHEN traveling, visit public and private mansions. They will inspire you and expand your vision.

$$ 356 $$

ALWAYS ask yourself what steps a great leader would take, then take them.

$$ 357 $$

WHEN leading a meeting, always bring your group to a consensus on as many issues as possible. This is critical to providing a unanimous accord that others will have difficulty challenging.

$$ 358 $$

LEADERS always accept 100 percent responsibility for themselves and their companies. They never blame others or criticize them. They are able to move forward rapidly because they see themselves as responsible for their circumstances and their results.

$$ 359 $$

THE more you speak to people as if they are capable, the more capable they will be.

$$ 360 $$

How you react to what is happening often has a greater effect than what actually happened. The higher your level of leadership skill, the more you replace inappropriate reaction with appropriate response.

$$ 361 $$

THE more comfortable you are with the unknown, the more trust you will develop in your intuitive senses. Leaders often stand in the un-known, and all leaders trust their intuition.

$$ 362 $$

CAPACITY problems can be physical and/or emotional. The former may be obvious and the latter more subtle; however, either one will prevent growth. An effective leader must consistently move all the blocks out of the way or the organization will stagnate.

$$ 363 $$

ALL character can be broken down into thousands of individual characteristics. To make your leadership behavior more effective, isolate specific characteristics and work persistently on changing, developing, and improving them, one at a time.

$$ 364 $$

KEEP your staff focused on the big picture, and you will hear fewer complaints.

$$ 365 $$

THE most profitable businesses are not necessarily those with the most skilled employees or the best products. They are the ones with the best marketing strategy and the best leadership.